READY, SET, NETWORK

Seven Keys To Unlocking Business Building Success

KC TOWNES, MA

Copyright © 2020 KC Townes, MA

ISBN 978-1-7355260-5-8 (paperback)
ISBN 978-1-7355260-6-5 (ebook)

JM Publishing

All rights reserved. No part of this book may be reproduced, stored, or transmitted by any means—whether auditory, graphic, mechanical, or electronic—without written permission of both publisher and author, except in the case of brief excerpts used in critical articles and reviews. Unauthorized reproduction of any part of this work is illegal and is punishable by law.

Printed in the United States of America

CONTENTS

Introduction vii

Dedication ix

Chapter 1: Let's Get 'Ready' (What if?) 1

Chapter 2: Now You are 'Ready' (What Comes Next) 9

Chapter 3: Get 'Set' (Choosing Your Business) 15

Chapter 4: 'Set' Your Business in Motion (Who
    do you trust?) 31

Chapter 5: You Are 'Set' to *W.I.N. (Who trusts me?) ... 43

Chapter 6: 'Network' to W.I.N. (Decide not to
    implode) 50

Chapter 7: 'Network' Is an Ongoing Process!
    (Choosing your successors) 66

In Ready, Set, Network, K.C. provides the blueprint for anyone looking to get off the sidelines and into the game of life. Whether you are just starting out, have been in the industry for years and are feeling stuck, or have been doing good but want to do great, this book delivers proven step-by-step strategies to help you achieve your dreams.

Jermain Miller
Founder of MiLL RE, CEO of Jermain Miller Consulting
3x Best Selling Author

Over the past nineteen-plus years, I have had the pleasure of observing KC coach and/or mentor thousands of people who aspire to become leaders in business. In this timeless book, KC carefully lays the foundation for entrepreneurs who are not only ready to put in the work to build a lasting legacy, but who also aim to pay it forward with compassion and empathy.

Jai A. Darden
Business Advisor, Professional Sales Trainer

"*Ready, Set, Network* is based on the author's decades of experience building organizations and, more importantly, building people. Network Marketing industry phenom K.C. Townes takes logical, practical principles, puts them in easy to apply language and gives the blueprint for success to the reader. Simply apply them and watch your business(es) soar!! A must-read for everyone in our industry."

Dr. Katrina Ferguson, CEO, Ultimate Coaching Exchange, Professional Networker and 4x Best Selling Author

If you truly want to change the direction of your economic life, it starts with purchasing this book. The inevitable outcomes that come from buying into the core tenets of the book are a testament to Mr. Townes's leadership and vision in providing a platform for entrepreneurs to plant their seeds, to harvest their crops, and to share the rewards of their labor

Dr. Chuck Herring, Co-Founder Herring Seminars and Consulting

KC Townes has a wealth of knowledge and real experience in our industry, and his ability to teach the information is phenomenal. I believe this book will make an impact on your life. Make sure you read it!!

Muzafer Najfi
Seven Figure Income Networking Earner

INTRODUCTION

Starting a business. Are there any three words that speak more to the idea of being free? I started my first home-based business in 1987 as a young man in the military stationed in Alaska. When I started, I had no hint of the incredible future that was now in front of me. What I knew about business was very little and pretty basic. I just knew I wanted more for the people I cared about. I was recently married, with young children who were dependent on us. I remember going to my first business meeting, unsure of what to expect. I vividly remember the fear that comes from being excited to be doing something I'd only dreamed of and the worry of it not working out. But I knew I wanted to make more money and get out of my situation.

The advice in this book will help you achieve the many benefits of becoming a successful small business entrepreneur. Personal development, time management mastery, meeting new interesting and exciting people, and world travel are just a few of the rewards that come

INTRODUCTION

from owning and operating a business. But to receive these incredible gifts, you must get started. That's what this book is all about—preparing you for the initial part of your success journey by uncovering some of the challenges and rewards associated with beginning your business.

Decide early to maintain a focus on the decision you made to launch your business. In the beginning, even the best networkers had no idea of the challenges they would encounter and eventually conquer. Because proper preparation normally results in a pleasing payoff, they were able to overcome and achieve.

Welcome to a life of more time and income freedom!

DEDICATION

It's funny how beginning a project like this book allowed me to reflect on all the lives I touched along the way—and all the people who have poured into me. My story is like so many other Networkers who experienced life-changing events along the way to 'It' happening. People shared things that didn't seem to mean a lot at the time, but their impact became more apparent as I continued my journey. I had no idea how many lives could be positively affected by simple conversations over coffee, in a hotel lobby or on the way home from a gathering.

This dedication is a thank you to some of the people who have poured into me as my life and personal growth were taking place.

My phenomenal parents, John and Caroline - I can't even express the Love and Lessons you poured into me. I can never pay you back, so I will help others with the gifts you have given me over these years. My life goal is to make you prouder

DEDICATION

To my siblings Jeff (Sharon) and Walter (Kelly) – A huge thanks for being loving, supportive, and family. Whatever and wherever, I'm there for you always.

To my big sister Trisha, love you and thanks for watching over me.

To the incredible Joe Watkins, my first business mentor, who took the time to pour into me when others passed on the opportunity.

To two of the people who became friends after we met in business, Jai and Nazir. This could not have happened without the two of you providing encouragement, support, friendship, and so much more. I know you're both saying - finally!

To Mike, Traci and Lil Mike - thanks for loving 'Unc' and taking care of Grandma, and so much more.

Dorothy! Hey girl, friendship and family for so long, love ya.

Maurice, thanks for always believing in 'Unc.' We are going to make it, believe that.

READY, SET, NETWORK

To Jon and Darrell - the friendship journey continues. Stay on your path, and we have so many more great times ahead.

To Doc, KB and Saleem - you're no longer here, but your love, sincerity and friendship I carry with me always.

I apologize to anyone I may be leaving out of this dedication who has shown me love, friendship and support. There are so many of you, so many events, so many places, and so many times you said or did just a little something that made all the difference between success or less. Here is my blanket hug to you all.

To my Internal Crew. I have the most incredible and supportive group on the planet. My thick and thin has been a reality for all of us, and you're still here by my side. I cannot express in words the amount of pride and love that's in me for all of you. Keith, Reshon', Donte', Cassie, Angie, Shawn, Asha, Dave and Ameer—I got your back because you have all had my front!! The best is yet to come.

And to the greatest gift you could ever share with me, my incredible grandchildren, Sequoia, Morgan, MaCory, Keith, Kai, Dashawn, Jaden, Aniyaha, Laila, Mariah, Greyson, Kadence and Lennox (more on the way). Since I started writing, we have been blessed to welcome Zuri and

DEDICATION

Luka, my Great-grand additions! Life starts over at Great Grandpop!

To my life partner, Lorraine. I have so much to say about our journey. Sharing, enduring, loving. We've endured getting through it, to continue to move to! And we continue to build our incredible story. Coming out on the other side is a blessing, and having you here still is the key to our enduring love story. Faith in the future, while never forgetting our past, is the launchpad to our ability to continuing, creating and succeeding. I LOVE YOU.

All my best

KC T

CHAPTER 1

Let's Get 'Ready' (What if?)

The buzzer just went off. It's time to roll, and you're wondering some of the things we've all wondered at one time or another in our business lives.

What if my dream doesn't work?

What if I'm not good enough?

What if I fail?

What if I find out this really isn't what I wanted to do in the first place?

These questions, as common as they are, will only take you off your success path. They will deliver you right back to the land of ordinary, black and white dreams. These questions do not focus on your goals and dreams actually coming true.

The word ordinary and the term black and white in the analogy both refer to ordinary thinking. Ordinary is what most people do. The masses do not practice the focus to equip them to be ready, set and network.

Rule #1 - If everyone is doing it, then do the opposite.

Why, you ask? After all, there are some great people here in this land of ordinary—people who you've known your whole life. In fact, the majority of people live in this land. However, long-term networkers are not here! They are obviously willing to do what others don't and won't.

As you travel on your success journey, the things you master to become successful do not require specialized degrees. No mystical or unique skills are needed, either. Anyone can achieve success in networking. This is one of the key reasons so many people are attracted to this industry of time and income freedom.

Rule #2 - Anything that is easy to do is easier not to do.

The masters in our industry, the top 3% income and lifestyle earners, will share that becoming successful is simple, but it is not easy. You must believe in yourself and follow through on the simple tasks that must get done, and that is not always easy. But without completing the tasks, you don't achieve your goal. The secret sauce is the effort, and that scares a lot of people. Most people are attracted to ease and comfort, not challenges.

If you are launching a business of your own, then you do not want to do what everyone does. The behaviors of the ordinary will yield you ordinary results. You want to duplicate behaviors that the insightful and successful networkers practice. Instead of following the crowd of ordinary, they blaze new trails for others to follow and find success in places the ordinary don't dare to go. Doing what everyone does is comfortable and safe, and staying comfortable and safe will get you what everyone has: a regular income with an ordinary lifestyle.

What is so bad about striving for ordinary? What is so bad about being comfortable finding safety in the crowd? Ordinary may be fine for some people, but it is not the place to achieve extraordinary results. Many of us already have ordinary, but you were looking for a change when you invested your money to begin your new business. You weren't happy with the return on your time investment, and you wanted more out of life.

LET'S GET 'READY' (WHAT IF?)

There is what I call a Land of In-Between. This land is based on your perceptions, formed from surrounding yourself with ordinary thinkers. The Land of In-Between is based on your fears and disappointments. In this land, you are no longer focused on building a business and utilizing your strengths. Fear is now driving your lack of business goals. The fact that the majority of new businesses often don't survive means there will be some ups and some downs on the way to your success. At this point, you're in between finding something else and just running in another direction. This is the place—right here—where you begin to rationalize: I don't know if this is for me?

So, how can you leave the Land of In-Between? What you need is a success strategy, a system that begins with awareness and builds momentum as you and your business grow. A strategy/system that helps you get stronger while practicing correct behaviors repeatedly, until you get it right. I remember being incredibly discouraged early in my networking career. I was getting ready to quit. I believed I was as good as any of the leaders I saw on the stages of the world. My 'comfort' (you know—lazy) mind started to kick in. It told me that things aren't fair. I also believed the leaders were getting special favors and gifts that I did not have access to. (Here is a clue that you are not feeling good about your business: you think the successful are all cheating or getting favors you cannot have.)

> *Tip: Ask yourself - What chance of success do you have with a mindset like the one I just shared?*
>
> *Have you or anyone you know ever had that same mindset, or worse?*
>
> *And of course, ask yourself - Who is the biggest enemy to your success, other people, or the enemy inside you who thinks this way?*

One of my mentors shared a philosophy with me that helped me toughen up and endure. She told me about the great Les Brown and his journey from being abandoned as an infant to becoming a world-class motivational speaker. I began purchasing his books, immediately reading as much as possible, and something that he said truly inspired and motivated me: 'Anything worth doing is worth doing badly, until you get it right.'

That one statement turned my ordinary attitude and my outlook around. It fortified my desire to go beyond simply wanting to become successful, because it meant like me, Les Brown had encountered disappointments too. More importantly, like Les Brown, I now understood the power of getting up!

Rule #3 - 'When life knocks you down, try to land on your back. Because if you can look up, you can get up.' - (Les Brown)

Reading Les Brown's works, I realized I was not the only person who had hit a wall in my first few business endeavors. Everyone has setbacks. Even more importantly, I knew like Les Brown, you and I can find a way to win. Remember—a setback is an indicator of desire and effort. It is a sign that you are working hard and meeting challenges along the way.

Rule #4 - Avoid anyone and everyone who ever said they've never failed! Never failing is an indicator of consistently not trying.

As I bring this chapter to a conclusion, I want to leave with the words of the great philosopher Lao Tzu: 'The journey of a thousand miles begins with the first step.' Your early disappointments in business, as long as you don't keep repeating them, are your first steps towards achieving your dreams.

I want to share a little secret. The first time you land on Disappointment Drive, the only person who potentially believes you failed is you. It feels horrible to you, but the rest of the world will not notice unless you inform them.

When you are confronted with disappointment, just keep driving forward and avoid going into reverse. From this point forward, stop asking for fewer hurdles to jump. Ask for the strength and patience to continue growing through your next business challenges. The reality is, if you stick to and stay on your success path, you are closer than ever before to achieving your goals, desires and dreams.

Doing the task means you only have two outcomes: success or gaining valuable experience. Average thinkers are afraid of trying to be successful. If they fall short, in their limited thinking, they believe a flaw in them has been exposed. This actually exposes one of their biggest flaws, which is insecurity. Visionary thinking allows you to understand why so many people who enroll or invest in a business will quit! It's not their business failing that creates doubt. It is the public revelation (everyone else's opinion) of the possibility of not hitting their target that scares them!

LET'S GET 'READY' (WHAT IF?)

Recap: Everyone is here for a different reason. Some of the people you know are going to excel in business building. Others are here to introduce you to the next big deal, the next influencer, or the next industry legend.

Be willing to accept that everyone you have met on your journey won't be there when you cross the stage and are recognized for your accomplishments.

Accept that all our success stories are different. Some are short, while others require more time. Viewing business this way will help you to accept this reality. It also helps you survive and endure when close friends, family and the people you have encouraged decide to stop striving. If you master this concept alone, you're prepared to endure and have a journey to success.

CHAPTER 2

Now You are 'Ready' (What Comes Next)

So now you know challenges are a natural (and essential) business reality. Endurance, patience and acceptance of the challenges ahead are some of the keys to you creating your success story. What comes next?

Once you're aware and accepting of the anticipated challenges, next you need to decide. The decisions you make early in your career will be keys to whether your industry impact is that of a Participant (along for the ride until you're discouraged or see something different) or a Player (having a long-lasting and legendary career). Those two P's are a reality, and where you end up often results from the decisions you made early in your networking career.

Rule #5 - What you do early duplicates late.

NOW YOU ARE 'READY' (WHAT COMES NEXT)

Any behavior practiced over and over becomes a habit. Positive habits practiced over and over can turn an ordinary life into a lifestyle. When you choose a positive and impactful leader/mentor to emulate, that decision will influence the behaviors you develop and practice, which ultimately create your habits. The great news is, you have committed to getting better, and you will.

Once you begin to follow the leader, there are a few *dos and don'ts* to remember:

1. Emulate the behaviors of someone who has what you want or who is committed to working on it with someone who has what you both want.

2. Be consistent. Do not follow multiple styles, beliefs and ideologies. This leads to confusion, and when you are in confusion, very little gets accomplished.

3. Remember, just because someone had success in another industry, regardless of how many millions they made, it does not guarantee they will be able to transfer that success to the industry you are a part of now.

4. There will be times when someone tells you about things you should do to achieve success. They give you

advice, even though you have never seen or heard them talk about doing the activities previously. They may be leveraging your enthusiasm (hard hat time) to see if the task will work. In other words, they know you're enthusiastic about working with them, so you must beware. Unless your goal is to be a crash test dummy, do not follow this person (notice I didn't say leader here).

5. The people you sponsor are going to watch what you do. Leadership is a 24/7 detail. Walk what you talk and be consistent. Have integrity.

As you can tell, much of what happens in business is grounded in belief and faith. You must have belief in the person you are following, mentoring with and buying into. Think about the people who believed in you throughout your life. People like your significant other, parents, grandparents, children, friends, etc. These are folks who know you will be honest. They believe you'll share things with them that have meaning, value and a positive impact.

I remember those cherished times when I would tell my two youngest children bedtime stories. I made up the stories and personalities that I shared with them night after night. After a while, my daughter asked me, 'Daddy, did you make these stories up?' When I told her yes, she wasn't disappointed. She wanted to hear more stories! Later, when my daughter was a teenager, she told me looking back she believed the stories were valuable to her learning and creativity. She even thanked me for the fun we had and appreciated those times we shared. That is an example of belief in the leader. Because of what she saw in me through those stories (amongst other things) over her short lifetime, I had established my credibility. She had faith she could grow and learn something from the stories I shared with the two of them.

So, the decision you make about who you follow is crucial. Not just important, it's crucial. Remember, as your life evolves into a lifestyle, the changes often depend on the people whose habits you emulate. Again, I want to point out here—early behaviors practiced over and over become your habits, positive or negative. The people you enroll in your business model will duplicate your behaviors. They believe you are sharing and modeling behaviors that will have value for them. The behaviors they see you practice daily will be copied. They believe what they are now practicing will help create a successful outcome for them. This is how crucial it is to pick the right mentor!

Even if you are a new successful business owner, people will follow you because you have a level of success they desire. This is very important to understand and accept.

Rule #6 - Leadership won't ask permission. It will pick you when you are ready, not when you request it. Accept the responsibility that goes along with your growth.

For anyone a bit nervous about being one of the leaders, this next point may calm you. Your first responsibility is to be a follower-leader. Is it possible to lead while you follow? It's not only possible, but we find the best leaders often began as the best followers.

The key is your ability to remain coachable, continue to listen, and follow those who have what you still desire through your growth. One of the things that can alter or delay your success path is believing at the beginning of your success that you are now done with the learning part of leadership and development. Nothing could be further from true. Business is a daily learning experience. Embrace the challenge to continually develop.

I hope you're beginning to get excited about all your future business possibilities, and realize that many have experienced what you are growing through.

NOW YOU ARE 'READY' (WHAT COMES NEXT)

> *Recap: Deciding early to be a Player or Participant will determine the level of success you rise to.*
>
> *Practicing great habits early often creates sustained great results. Leaders understand behaviors, both great and not so great, repeated over time will become habits. Your focus should be on duplicating the productive behaviors of successful people who have what you want. If you copy them, the people in your organization will duplicate the positive behaviors you're practicing.*

CHAPTER 3

Get 'Set' (Choosing Your Business)

Once you realize and believe in the concepts we've covered, you're about halfway to creating a strong, solid launch for your business. Choosing the company you want to be aligned with and what industry you want to represent is your next step. You might be saying, 'Picking a company or industry is the easy part.' That's sometimes true. There are, however, multiple internal conversations you will have on the road to making a solid business decision. So, what is a solid business decision?

A solid decision means first you have aligned yourself with a company you intend to be a part of for a significant amount of time. So the next question is: What is considered a significant amount of time? Well, that depends on your 'Why'—why you enrolled in the industry and company you represent. Some of the more influential people in the world buy and sell companies every year. A few purchase

GET 'SET' (CHOOSING YOUR BUSINESS)

and invest in different companies monthly. For people at this level of influence, a significant amount of time is considerably different from the average person's perception. A significant stretch of time for a new business owner is normally going to be anywhere from one to three years. If you've owned multiple successful businesses, then a significant amount of time is again different based on a different set of concerns.

This decision will vary based on your drive and motivational needs. Your focus may be to own the business for one year or less, if that's how long you believe it will take you to meet your goals. Now, take a moment and determine your most important reasons for being a small business owner. Your goals will include building benchmark income that achieves two things. First, it creates the amount of revenue required to satisfy your 'Why.' And second, it creates the type of income that can influence others to join you in your business endeavor. Your networking or business home should provide you with a desirable amount of time and income freedom.

Rule #7 - Just because someone owns a traditional business, it does not mean they have time or income freedom.

Many business owners will tell you their business owns them. Remember, there are expenses not required in networking businesses, such as employees, insurance, rent, furnishings, the need to be at the location during business hours and beyond, payroll and security, just to name a few.

The next point regarding making a solid decision is to pick a company that satisfies an internal (not just income) motivational drive. It's important to your longevity to have an affinity with the company you choose. I am referring to the internal desires like real belief in the product or service you market. Be a product of your products, and use them yourself. Share honest testimonials of the results you've witnessed for yourself and others. Sharing the positive impact your service or product has on the environment or a group of people is important.

These reasons are solid and long-lasting. When others ask you why you're marketing or selling your service or products, your response should have conviction! This conviction will help insulate you from the skeptics and negative people who may be asking questions based on their lack of belief. You'll also begin having monetary satisfaction when you sell your products or market your services. Regardless of what motivates you, your enrollment decision is incredibly important.

So let's get to the task at hand. How do you decide which company to enroll in?

GET 'SET' (CHOOSING YOUR BUSINESS)

I would like to begin by saying that business leaders use an incredibly effective common-sense formula when picking a company. But the truth is, many times, your company picks you. For example, you may have a friend in a company, and they invite you to a meeting or gathering. Because your friend is enrolled in that company, joining seems like the right thing to do. Or maybe you weren't looking for a business opportunity, and someone invited you to a gathering. You saw people enrolling, and you decided you did not want to be left out. There are times when someone you respect influences you to enroll. You're sitting there, next to a very accomplished person. They turn to you after the presentation and say, 'Of course, you're not obligated, but if I were you, (here it comes) I would get involved in this thing right now, while it's a great time.' You have no clue what to do. The reality is, you don't want to look like you have no clue, so you enroll. Then, three months later, you quit because you still have no clue what to do or why you joined. Your sponsor never says anything to you. They get their bonus, you get to say you were in business with the big shot, blah, blah, blah, and life goes on.

Here's the big-picture view of what just happened. That person hurt the industry's future chances of ever attracting you and all the good things you can bring to the industry. Their actions also perpetuate the negative myths that used to (and sometimes still) define our industry.

The truth is, most people, especially early on, have no idea how to choose a company. Most people believe that the four-letter dirty word, 'Luck,' has much to do with leaders' success. If luck means being in the right place at the right time, then the answer is yes. If luck means the harder we work, the luckier we get, then I guess these are examples of luck. But you can't count on luck. At this point, I hope you decide to enroll because of your passion and belief in the company, service or products you market and represent.

Belief and passion help you develop long-term focus and drive. The truth is, everyone won't enroll for the reasons I just mentioned. So, what comes first, the chicken or the egg? Your decision to enroll is a lot like this rhetorical question.

What came first, your passion for the business, products and services, or the promise of riches and success? The decisions along the way to building your business will depend on what's inside of you: your makeup, needs, and what was important in your life when you decided to enroll and become a small business owner. There's no magic button to push to get your business machine moving forward. Success will be the coming together of the little bits of everything you do consistently.

GET 'SET' (CHOOSING YOUR BUSINESS)

Success is also about the people you pay attention to and the things you choose to ignore. There will continue to be dozens of factors contributing to the outcome of your efforts. Because so much of your success is dependent on your internal drive, moods and who influences you, chronicle as much of your journey as possible. One thing I know about your success journey is, it will inspire the people you enroll, and even people you don't know are watching!

Rule #8 - Not everyone you inspire will be in your organization.

Not everyone you inspire will be on your team, and some may not live in your area. Diving deeper into influence, some people you inspire won't even be in the networking industry. Just remember, as you grow, so does your legend and the number of people who are impacted by what you say, do and have accomplished. People don't always like to hear this, because this means your positive and not so positive outcomes can influence others.

Here's a subtle and often not discussed fact: Some people (not leaders) only want the income they work to create. They don't want everyone watching the outcomes of their activity. They haven't accepted, nor do they want, the responsibilities that go along with leadership. They may have forgotten when they themselves were watching the behavior of leadership that was modeled for them. Or, they may have forgotten the steps required to obtain their time and income freedom.

Rule #9 - Never forget, much of the success you experience results from watching and duplicating the activities and outcomes of others.

The time and income freedoms you achieve are noticeable commodities. Just like you watched and learned from the freedom behaviors of others, everyone is now watching how you created freedom for yourself. Remember to trust a short pencil to a long memory as you document your journey, and be sure to keep the story factual, real, inspirational and accurate.

Now let's talk about business passion, which means you're doing what you enjoy. Passion is a simple, seven-letter word, but in business, the impact of being passionate about what you do is huge. The success this industry provides empowers you to be one of the privileged few on the planet who is living your life dream. In this industry, 'working' happens while you're leading others, which is an investment in your lifestyle.

GET 'SET' (CHOOSING YOUR BUSINESS)

Ask yourself, 'What work do I really want to do for the rest of my life?' With this as your focus, take this survey on work satisfaction:

1. Before starting your business, people asked you what you wanted to do for a living. What was your answer? *The real answer. You know, the dream.* This is your 'Why.'

2. Did you want to follow in the footsteps of a relative or someone who is like family? Someone who made an impression on you as you were growing up? Why did/do you want to be like them? Picking the best mentors is crucial!

3. What was it they did or said that attracted you to them? Is it still attractive today?

4. Have you thought about picking up and pursuing that calling since then? Reach out for guidance throughout your journey.

5. If you chase that dream, is it for you or to satisfy someone else? Think about what we discussed regarding your passion.

6. To pursue your dream now, what will it take? Time, commitment, money, support from others, etc.? This is the sacrifice part. Sacrifice is a part of your story, and this is what you use to inspire others on their journey!

7. Will you have to rely on the help of others to achieve the goal? No worries, teamwork can make your dream work. Even the best leaders needed assistance, so check your ego early.

8. Once you achieve the success you desire, what will you do for others? What will you do for yourself? You get what you want by helping others get what they desire!

9. Who else will benefit from your success? How many lives you touch is a part of your payoff.

10. Have you set the date of your success achievement? (Day, month and year. Be specific!) You must have a real 'When' to accompany your 'Why.'

Now that you have answered the questions, do you have a clearer view of what drives you to want success? Are you in touch with what motivates you? Was your dream created from something you saw others achieve?

GET 'SET' (CHOOSING YOUR BUSINESS)

Quick Task: On a piece of paper, write down the answers you just came up with on the left side. Next to the answers, on the right side, write down what you will need to do to make your goals a reality.

When you choose a company to be a part of, that company represents your pathway to achieving the goals you wrote down. Even though we may share some universal dreams and goals, everyone's path to success will be unique. What motivates me may not be the thing that motivates you. What your neighbor needs to work on to have success is not the same thing your cousin needs to have the same measure of success. Money doesn't motivate everyone. Some people enjoy the journey to achieving their dreams, while others may enjoy a little of both. Choose your company wisely. Make your goals and dreams a key part of how you choose the company that positions you for the success you desire.

Now, review the self-assessment you just completed. The left side represents your goals and desires; the right side represents what you need to be successful. As you review the chart, take note of the things that inspire you to want success. Develop an understanding of what motivates you. If it's your needs that motivate you, then it is the survival part of your success equation that drives you. Things like mortgage, food, daycare, paying your electric bill, maybe medical coverage, life insurance—the list is infinite. If you're motivated by your wants and desires, then it is important to understand that great new vehicle, the fancy coat or suit, the once-in-a-lifetime vacation and other life extras are what lights your motivational fire.

When you think about the people you have known throughout your life, chances are some of them want success based on their needs, while others are motivated by their wants. Both sides are equally passionate. I have heard people say, "This doesn't make sense. If I must feed my family, no one could possibly want luxury just as much as my desire for survival." I have also heard people explain how needing something to survive is important, but it can't be as important as something they've worked their whole life to acquire.

Decision priority is derived from what is important to you.

Remember, wants and desires are a part of everyone's makeup. There's no universal description of what everyone considers important, whether it is survival, motivational or life-changing. Hence the phrase 'Everything is not for everybody.' It's important to understand your motivators. When you have no clue what motivates you or why you are in a business, your great business launch can get derailed. Having no idea what inspires you or the people you enroll or hire means you have no idea what to do or say to motivate yourself or others! When the natural challenges arise, you'll end up unsure how to navigate past them.

Who you are is based on where you were when. This is one of the most overlooked aspects of creating early success in your business. The area you were raised in, the decade you grew up in, your parents' income level, the school system you were educated in, the friends you hung around, and your family all affect your thought process. These things (and so much more) all have a driving influence on how you view others. They will affect your willingness to reach across the aisle to communicate, attract, relate and share with people.

Two children are in the same sixth-grade class, sit side by side and are the exact same age. One child is raised by their parents in their thirties. The other is raised by their grandparents in their sixties. Their teacher gives them an assignment to ask their parents about a typical day when they were growing up in the sixth grade. Even though they both are in the same class, they are the same age and sit across from each other, the stories they bring to the class the next day are very different. How their guardians perceive life is based on where they were when. Growing up in the decade of the 2000s was totally different than growing up in the 1970s. The grandparents may talk about bell-bottoms, platform shoes or the popularity of tie-dye clothing. The parents may share stories about MTV, low-rise jeans, Myspace social networking or *American Idol*. When the sixth-graders share the stories, they are completely different. What shaped their thought and perception processes is different. As a result, how they assess similar events in their lives is different. Neither is wrong or right, and the same is true for you and me.

Understanding what influences you helps determine who you are and makes communicating across 'people differences' less challenging. Knowing that people have different motivators will make it easier to understand the drivers that keep people motivated to win. So again, it doesn't matter if you're driven mostly by your needs or by your desires. What is important is you, the new business owner, understand which value is driving your desire to succeed. Knowing your 'Why' is one of the keys to finishing your pursuit of successful business ownership!

Satisfying your needs and wants is vital to your future success. But even when their desires are clear, many people still get discouraged quickly and quit because of a few disappointments. Unless you've owned a business, it is difficult to internalize the highs and lows of being a business owner. The freedoms associated with being a successful networker or business owner often come with both recognition and responsibility.

GET 'SET' (CHOOSING YOUR BUSINESS)

Sometimes people decide to stop working on their dreams. They think, "Ah, the good life is here. I can relax." Some will simply quit, lacking the willingness to accept responsibility. And some quit because they are not passion motivated and are unsure why they are here.

Rule #10 - As your organization grows, the Pareto Principle (80/20 rule) will become more evident.

The Pareto Principle states that people will come and go, but only about 20% of those who enroll will be around when the success begins to kick in. It doesn't matter if the desire to quit happens immediately or if it takes a few months. When someone decides to leave, you only have a small window of time to get them turned around and refocused. You must help them refocus on 'Why' they decided to launch their business.

I'm often asked for two things when it comes to someone launching their business—my advice and my opinion. I have the same consistent answer all the time: "My opinion really doesn't matter, because I formulate that based on my wants and needs, not yours." Have you noticed that sometimes when you ask someone for their honest opinion, they give you their opinion of how you should do something to become successful? But it doesn't always work out for you, even though it worked out for them.

My advice is normally the same, start your business once you are ready and just get going. Don't ask for permission (employment mindset). Your being here, your eagerness and desire—those things are all the permission you need to start and succeed. The desires that burn in you are your pathway to freedom. They're based on your beliefs formed from your personal importance platform, built on what you've seen consistently throughout the years. Knowing your 'why,' staying focused, hungry and remaining coachable are your keys to open the front door of your success residence.

Next, the disappointments we spoke of earlier are going to happen. They're a natural part of your success journey. In my video series *Ready, Set Network*, I share the steps to building a firm foundation for your business success. Having a firm foundation is critical to your future success and growth. I cannot stress enough the importance of your foundation being anchored, solid and secure. In our industry, everyone who enrolls does not have the internal drive and stamina needed to withstand the emotional rollercoaster that's a part of our business environment. But like the butterfly that emerges after ten days in its cocoon, challenges are necessary to build the grit needed to endure and succeed.

You must sharpen your skills to motivate and lead others now and into the future. Leaders learn how to model for

GET 'SET' (CHOOSING YOUR BUSINESS)

others when they go through similar challenges. This is all a part of your essential system of Networking success.

> *Recap: Let's discuss your keys to making an educated decision when choosing a company.*
>
> *The amount of time you want to spend representing your chosen company depends on your personal situation and what drives you.*
>
> *Remember your business likes, needs and desires are decided by you. You also need to decide what amount of earned income will be your benchmark.*
>
> *Study the self-assessment in this chapter for a better understanding of what motivates and drives you.*
>
> *Finally, accept that 20% of your organization will carry the productivity load, and there will be some disappointments along your way to success.*

CHAPTER 4

'Set' Your Business in Motion (Who do you trust?)

Two questions come up time and time again when discussing the issues of trust and business building.

Many people do not have a firm understanding of how important trust is when building a business. They look at the businesses around them, both small and large, through the eyes of a static black-and-white thinker. They believe most people walk in, purchase things, and have no relationship with the business owner. They may wonder, "Why would trust matter?"

Static thinkers believe traditional business dictates anyone can buy anything from anyone. Our industry of networking is many things, but the best networkers are not static thinkers. This industry beckons freethinking people who stay up late wishing, hoping and dreaming. You share your wishes, hopes and dreams with people you relate to and know. Those folks tell you how much they believe in your future success. This helps give you the strength to start a business, which can lead to the launch of your incredible success story. So, your 'trust' core is relationships, the ones you have now, and those you will share with others in the future.

Our industry is relationship-driven, so who you decide to put your trust in is important. The people you trust often want you to win! These are the people who will embrace your drive to succeed, unlike the corner store traditionalist who does not need to have a relationship with you. Some of you reading this may say, "Well, it appears they have it easier. They can just open their doors and sell to anyone, so why don't I just open a store or franchise?" Remember the leverage advantage within the networking industry. Traditionalists need property, employees, insurance, furnishings, security and inventory, among other things. Unlike the corner store, much of your success is based on sharing concepts in the corner of your kitchen or backyard. Our industry is all about leveraging personal space, personal time and personal relationships.

When we talk about the people we trust, the accepted term is your 'warm market.' Your warm market is the folks you know, love and trust. Your 'cold market' is the people you do not know (yet). Warm market folks have known you for a lifetime and will continue to know you, regardless of what business model you represent. You will have a relationship with them for a major part of your lifetime. We often say these are the people in your inner circle.

In my video series, *Ready, Set, Network*, a guide to building a firm foundation for your networking business, I discuss the difference between your warm and cold markets, and why they are not cold or warm. I use more descriptive terminology because of the importance and impact of trust on your immediate and future growth. I refer to your trusted (warm) and respected (cold) markets and the importance of understanding the differences in both when it comes to business building.

Business building, while simple in concept, is sometimes not easy. Still, it is a science that anyone can master. But along the way, you'll need some glue to hold your business together. Until the foundation settles and it becomes firm, the glue that holds your structure together is trust. I'm not talking about casual *I think I trust you* trust. I'm talking about *I trust you with my wallet, with the well-being of my family, with the things that mean the most to me* trust. Think about it; you are building your business to take care of the people you care about. That type of business building is not casual. It can get intense and it can be challenging, but when business building and trust come together, it's also incredibly rewarding.

So, what's required for you to develop trust while building your business? You will need an initial criterion—a benchmark. You should establish a criterion that is important to you.

Rule #11 - Trust is an area in which others will often share advice based on their experiences.

Acknowledge their concerns and criteria, but make trust decisions based on your values. They mean well, but there is an old saying: What I eat doesn't affect your waistline. In other words, just because someone you know doesn't like or trust someone else doesn't mean it applies to you.

Rule #12 - If trust is an issue for more than one person, then that is considered a trend. And if it is, pay attention to the advice being given.

I think you would agree the things you and I base our trust on will not always be the same. You base your trust on things that are important to you, and the same is true for me. The criteria for trust are based on our experiences, those things we've experienced dealing with people and how people have dealt with us. Remember, who you are is based on where you were when.

Take a moment and write down the names of ten people you consider trustworthy. Remember, these are the people you want to become the glue in the foundation of your business. This glue will be strong enough to hold your structure together until your foundation is firm. It will be strong enough to keep your business productive for years to come.

While you're taking notes, factor in the Pareto Principle—the 80/20 rule. This means out of those ten people you trust, eight will look at your business model, listen to your story and understand it, but they won't fully engage. You may think, "I know at least half of my people will become customers or enroll, and that's five new people right there." You're sincere in your resolve and focus on building with these new business partners you trust. But here is a business building fact you need to know: this group of future business partners may get started and then enroll in your business. But starters are a dime a dozen, and you are not looking for starters. It's finishers you are looking for. So out of the ten who enrolled, a safe average is two of these same ten people will finish the journey with you.

Rule #13 - Always remember, finishers will complete the journey with you, but they did not stay for you!

Finishers are building their own dreams and reaching for their own goals. The people they enroll are not here for them either. Their individual wishes, desires and goals keep them hungry and driven. It's a person's personal goals that keep them focused and solid while they are working to fulfill their dreams!

No matter how long you stay or how far you travel in your business career, the Pareto Principle is a reality. The powerful thing about our industry is, it's not just about you. Here's a practical example for you. Of those ten who originally enrolled in your organization, if just five of them enrolled one person each, you have ten new business partners. Why not fifteen, you ask? Because I'm focusing on your active business partners. Remember, in this example, five of your ten partners enrolled one new partner. You now have a total of ten active partners. If two of these five new business partners are as serious as you are, and each enrolled ten each, you now have a total of 27 active partners. Remember, some will stay active and some won't, but the constant is systemic productive growth! To realize your dream and the dream-building process, it is wise to accept the impact of the Pareto Principle. It's the law of business and life.

Rule #14 - Human nature is the cornerstone for relationships, but not business building.

I have discussed who will stay in your business, but it is equally important to discuss who you invest your time with. If you enroll your friend in your business, you have a vested interest in being there for them. Understanding this friendship rule is vitally important. If your friend begins to slow down or stop business building, human nature tells you to slow down and start investing your time to help them get back on what you believe is their track. The normal human tendency is to want to save them, because they are your friend. Yes, you should try to get them going again. Yes, you should invest some time trying to get them refocused and back on track. You should not, however, spend a great deal of time doing this.

What is a great deal of time, you ask? Don't invest more time working with them than you do with the people who are committed and working. I used two different terms here: investing and working. The time you spend getting your friend back on track is work. The time you spend with the people who are focused and producing is an investment.

Where you focus your time is as important as the decision you made to enroll.

Rule #15 - Work where you're deserved, not where you are needed.

Focus on working with the willing. Think about this. Have you ever had a business partner who had an event at their home or office? A lot of people showed up, and it felt great. During the event, people really liked the information, products and services. The people at this event openly showed interest. As a result, you're as excited as if you had hosted this event yourself. When the event is over, people leave. No one enrolls or purchases anything, but you know tomorrow or the next day, great things are going to happen because of this event.

There are a couple of points here. First, those of us that have been active have all been there. This is a part of your learning and growth curve. After the event, you went back to your mentor and asked what you should've done differently. Your mentor gave you the secret sauce, the missing ingredients. Now you know how to turn an event into productive time spent and not wasted time (investment vs. work).

Now you meet with the distributor who hosted the event to discuss the sacred 'secret sauce.' You begin to share with them, and as you start, you see that look. They cut you off and begin sharing their disappointment about the event not delivering the wealth and success they anticipated. Then they drop it on you that, after talking to their significant other, this thing doesn't work. They share how they want to slow it down because people said "No" or "Not Now."

Because of their post-event outlook and attitude, you decide, "Man, I need to work with them." You begin spending time with them, taking them to get coffee and calling them at least once a day. This goes on for a while because you know if they hosted a big event once, they could do it again. (But do they want to do it again, and are they willing to find out how to do it more effectively?)

You are also spending time with them because you two have a relationship. You believe if you do not help them, you are not a good friend. Everyone who's been willing to grow out of their comfort zones and build a business has been there. It's the natural human tendency to want to rescue people you care about.

However, the business outlook side doesn't fall in line with the human emotional side. Spend time with people who are coachable, committed, working and focused. Spend your time with the partners who are positive and productive in their intention and results. When you follow this guidance, your time is now productive because it results in a return on your investment (ROI). That return (profit) is the reason you do the business.

Again, let me be clear here, continue to care for and spend time with the friend who quit or slowed down. Just don't waste the time you set aside to do your business to save them!

Who you decide to trust is one of my favorite areas to discuss, because the decision you make can take your business to its greatest heights! Unfortunately, misplaced trust decisions often result in nonfulfillment of your goals and dreams. You now know you'll need relationships to build a solid book of business. You know success is not dependent on just you.

Successful business building in our Networking industry is dependent on the efforts of the collective group. The people you really need are the people with whom you have a sincere trust. Remember that trust is based on your personal criteria, not the criteria of others.

Here's why this system of trust works so well in Networking: When you invest time with people you trust, helping to build their dreams, they are simultaneously building your dreams too! Using teamwork to make your dream work is one of the most rewarding parts of our industry!

Rule #16 - When you help others realize their goals and dreams, the same efforts simultaneously help build your dreams.

Another way of looking at this is—when you help others get what they want, you end up getting what you want too!

Your trust criteria aren't based on what your mentor believes or what the person who enrolled you in your business believes. It is not dependent on what your parents or siblings feel is important. Trust is based on what has value to you. As you discovered in this chapter, most of the people you share your dreams with won't be there for the entire journey. They may not be the ones who help you develop your business. They may not be there at the finish line when your dream is accomplished, and your life has now become a lifestyle. If they're not going to be there for the entire journey, how much time should you continue to spend with them?

Don't change your relationships with the people in your inner circle. The focus here is spending your business time with those who've earned it. Maintain those valuable sincere relationships while forging ahead to help whoever deserves your time to accomplish success!

'SET' YOUR BUSINESS IN MOTION (WHO DO YOU TRUST?)

Recap: Remember, trust means much more in a business driven by relationships. The people who trust you are your biggest fans.

Don't allow friendship to dictate who you invest your business time with.

When things don't go exactly as planned, that's not a reason to have a time-greedy pity party.

You reward people who are coachable and positive by sacrificing your time to help them. Put together an action plan to work with people who are deserving of your precious time.

CHAPTER 5

You Are 'Set' to *W.I.N. (Who trusts me?)

*What's Important Now

Rule #17 - Amateurs recruit, while professionals sort.

Recruiting is convincing. Sorting is exposing your prospect to your service, product or business model. Sounds kind of business romantic, right? When you are exposed to a business, service or product, the job of the person exposing you is to share a snapshot of that company's business plan. When this happens, the company you're being exposed to may appear to be the perfect fit for you.

I once began building a business with a great track record in a multibillion-dollar industry. Even though on the surface everything seemed ideal, I still had some doubts. My concern wasn't focused on the company. My concern was centered on the individual who exposed me to the business model. He sounded good, looked impeccable, and he even smelled great. In other words, he appeared to be the right person to partner up with.

However, I was uncomfortable partnering up with someone that most of the people around him had trust issues with. As a leader in this company, he didn't show faith in the people he entrusted to develop and help grow the company he wanted me to enroll in! In business, this is a real possibility. Sometimes, people in leadership positions have a business style that doesn't attract you, even though they have accomplished some of what you want. Their style creates second-guessing. Second-guessing in business creates doubt. Doubt in your leadership can impact your passion when you share your business with others. When you doubt someone, it can lead to negative trust issues that can capsize your business before it really gets started!

If you're in business with someone who has trust issues with you, you can expect limited to no support. In our relationship-driven industry, people need to develop trust in you to justify investing their time with you. That trust is incredibly important to your business development and future industry success.

Let me share some common examples of how you'll need the trust and support of others throughout your networking career. This industry is built on stories—incredible stories of overcoming obstacles and hurdles along your way to achieving success. The unique way we build trust and respect in our industry is through a key component called edification. Edification is the simple but effective art of sincerely speaking well of someone else. Edification is a behavior not traditionally practiced in business.

Here is a classic example of edification: You just launched your new business, and you don't know much yet about your new industry. Since you enrolled, you've been running on adrenaline and excitement, which attracts a lot of people. People enroll and invest thousands to be a part of what you do. All this happens based on your excitement and enthusiasm. You have the passion and energy that comes with having hope your life will be positively impacted by enrolling in your new company. You want others to know about your new opportunity. You want them to become motivated to enroll because of your anticipated successes. So, you begin sharing what you heard and saw up to this point, and people are drawn to your excitement.

The point here is, as you grow in our relationship-based industry, people will edify you and your story. This edification builds belief in others to enroll in your business and purchase services and products. Now, you no longer rely on excitement and energy as your key business tools. People begin to believe in you and ask about your business model because of the changes they witness in your lifestyle! This is when business building becomes enjoyable and even fun. Your results are now beginning to become predictable. People are also beginning to talk about what you are accomplishing.

But if there is no belief and trust in you, people won't edify or say kind words about you and what you bring to the business. The parts of the business you understand, you are excited about. In my trainings, seminars and mentorship groups, I talk about the four levels of conscious learning. The first level is Unconscious Incompetence. It is common in all business circles and simply means you don't know what you don't know. And at this point in your career, it's okay not to be the expert. But at some point, you will need to understand your business more deeply to build trust and edification.

So, what helps you build the type of success that motivates people to begin edifying your story? One of the keys is what you are doing right now: personal development. The books you read, the lessons you listen to, the seminars you attend and more are critical in your personal, business and trust development.

Rule #18 - Edification is an effortless art you need to master to become one of our industry legends.

When someone speaks positively about the success you're having and the integrity of the people you do business with, it's much easier for your prospects to make their decision to enroll!

A few key points here. First, you don't have to work as hard as the people who had success before you. You're becoming 'sticky,' and people will start asking you about your business, products or services.

Next, new distributors are normally curious about what to do next. They enroll with a coachable mindset, which shortens their learning and success curve. They're not arguing with you about "The way we do it on my job." When they have success quicker, you can share (edify) their story faster. Now your organization has created a positive success trend, which instills the belief that anyone can become successful! This is the impact of adding edification and creating a success system. When an effective system begins to impact an organization, it grows bigger, better and faster. It means no one person must be everywhere, doing everything for the team to win! This is HUGE. Speaking well of others creates an excitement that is a key part of business building, making it more predictable and fun!

Edification is the backbone of our networking industry. It has so much to do with the critical trust factor people develop, which is reinforced by your excitement and belief in what you are doing and sharing. The trust others have in you is everything. In *Ready, Set, Network,* I devote two entire video chapters to the importance of building your story and how to effectively share it with the world. The trust people have for you is never overstated. It is key to building your industry legend!

Here are three tips to effectively share your story:

1. Make sure you trust the person whose story you share with others (and of course, others will need to trust you too). Legitimacy and honesty are vital.

2. When you tell someone's story

    – Write it down
    – Rehearse in a mirror
    – Stand up when you practice
    – Check with others who are a part of the story for accuracy
    – Leave out the embarrassing parts, if possible
    – Keep it short, under one minute
    – Tell the story no less than 2-3 times daily
    – Take note of the effect your story has on others
    – Don't use names without permission

3. Unless you are asked, do not edify yourself. Let others tell your story. Become a master of telling other people's stories. When you lead with your story, you may be perceived as boastful, diminishing trust and effectiveness.

> *Recap: Make edification a habit.*
>
> *Practice saying things of significance daily while you're growing and learning.*
>
> *Accept that the people in your organization have four levels of competence. Know the value of the first level of unconscious incompetence, when excitement and enthusiasm will energize prospects to activity and initial launch success.*
>
> *When you practice your stories, stand. It increases your energy level.*
>
> *Track your enrollment results. Is this a story you should be sharing because it gets results, or is it simply entertaining?*

CHAPTER 6

'Network' to W.I.N. (Decide not to implode)

There's no doubt trust is enormous in any business or networking environment. I have focused two chapters of this book on the topic of trust. The trust you have for others, and the trust others have for you. Now it's time to focus on blazing your success trail. It's time to claim your victory, but be careful about some of the obvious—and not so obvious—pitfalls on the way to building your success story.

I'm talking about making the decision—a very conscious decision—that you will not implode. Some of you may be thinking, "Do you mean explode because I'm growing so fast?" No, I mean an implosion caused by things you should avoid, but instead, you've created them. In this case, what you create is not good for your business or you.

Let me share two very similar success examples: I know someone who worked a full-time job his whole life. There were times he worked two jobs, full- and part-time. Many people do this to support a family and pay the bills. There were also times he worked two jobs while attending college in his spare time. He did this hoping his efforts would earn him success. He hoped to get discovered by someone and get hired in his dream job because of his education, work ethic or desire to succeed. Along the way, he was also involved in network marketing, though he'd not achieved a lot of success. He hadn't made benchmark money. But he put everything into learning the tenants of business building, and he sat at the feet of some of the most brilliant networking minds of their time.

His break finally came after twelve years of laboring in full- and part-time jobs, attending school and immersing himself in learning the business of networking. He not only went to the top position in his company, but he also became a top 3% money earner. Now, after all that hard work, dedication and sacrifice, you'd think his focus would be centered around his next million, next big car, next house, a luxury vacation or other extravagant things. But when I interviewed him and asked what he spent most of his time focused on regarding business, he discussed two main areas.

'NETWORK' TO W.I.N. (DECIDE NOT TO IMPLODE)

First, he talked about how to get better at helping others achieve success. He said, "It's not about me, it's about how many lives I impact positively from today on." He focused on creating freedom for others! His other concern was building a legacy that edifies appreciation for the success his organization achieves. His focus was not on how good today is, but on how great tomorrow can be.

Wow! is the response I hope just came from you. (It was my response as he shared with me). In this interview, both of us grew, and this interview stretched me. It made me open up my mind to the reality of the impact success can have on others. You'll expand along with others, even if you're not ready for success when it arrives.

This next story is very similar, with a few exceptions. The second person worked full-time as a laborer. He didn't go to college. On multiple occasions, he attended trade school to further his technical expertise. He enrolled in an organization I was a part of, and I had the great fortune to mentor him over a little more than two years. I met with him personally at least three times a month. His success was achieved much quicker than the first individual. When we discussed his 'Why' and where he put his business focus, his answer was completely different. It was focused around the success he'd achieved, along with his earned income.

He asked me on more than one occasion, "KC, what if all this went away?"

I spent hours in the mental lab with him, discussing his earned success. I helped him focus on how fortunate he was to have so many capable and hardworking people in his organization. Just as important, I shared with him how much he deserved everything he'd achieved because of his hard work.

He would agree with me while we were together, but when he left me for a few days, his mindset went back to *What if this all went away.* He would often discuss his own business demise, and his focus was on the few negative occurrences that happened in his business. He used to tell me, "KC, I came up poor, so if I lose everything, I know I can make it." My response to his words was consistent: "Why are we focused on you losing everything you've earned and deserve? Focus on the things you visualized, worked hard for and are now a reality in your life. Why do we spend so much time talking about negative occurrences when your life and lifestyle are the type so many people desire and worked hard for just like you did?"

I asked him to mentally travel in the shoes of the people who looked up to him. Our conversation focused on him understanding his responsibility to continue seeking

'NETWORK' TO W.I.N. (DECIDE NOT TO IMPLODE)

success, not failure. This negative mentality is what my father used to call 'Seeking to fail.'

This is common in many people who come from a family where no tradition of success exists. Over time, they begin convincing themselves they really should live on Lack of Prosperity Lane. They believe they belong there, and to galvanize their thinking, they talk about the people they knew or know now who live in this same negative mental neighborhood. When they have success, it causes a level of discomfort and uncertainty. They find it easier to rationalize outwardly. They're prepared to possibly lose the great things they worked for.

There is an old saying, 'What you put out in the universe is what comes back to you.' This is also known as the Self-fulfilling Prophecy. In many cases, this prediction comes to fruition. The individual convinces themselves they're correct in not deserving the things they've achieved.

Rule #19 - Surround yourself with people who have a positive mental picture.

Surrounding yourself with positive thinking people who believe in you is essential when you're launching a business. Remember, you're working on achievement, which requires growth and change. Keep people around you who talk, carry themselves and think with a 'can do' outlook. They will raise your belief in whatever you are pursuing!

Many times, what surrounds 'seek to fail' people is a negative circle of influence. They're surrounded by people who question if success is deserving, real or will last. As a result, their language is a byproduct of the people around them. They become comfortable over time not believing great things will continue to happen for them. I have even heard some of these folks use the dreaded L-word—luck—when referring to their careers. This self-fulfilling personal prophecy of non-abundance becomes more powerful than the success they've achieved. It can even have a residual effect on the lives of the people in their trusted market. They hear the constant questioning and uncertainty of the success achieved by this networker. They no longer speak positive affirmations for themselves and quit believing they can have success. They now speak the language of uncertainty. No longer is positive reinforcement a daily occurrence. Instead, uncertainty is the language of the day.

Many of the most successful businesspeople I've met, have at one point, come to a mental decision fork in the road. A place where they wonder if it's worth continuing because of a challenge that presented itself. Some businesspeople achieve great things, then without explanation, they lose it all and have nothing. When a person is a victim of 'seek to fail' mentality, they begin unconsciously planning their demise.

Networkers are as apt to be a victim of this mentality as traditional business owners. Remember, we are the sum total of what surrounds us. We speak the language of the books we read, the places we go and the people we associate with. So, how do you keep this from happening to you?

There are three ways to insulate ourselves from seeking to fail:

First, there is the Aggressive Approach, which means you choose to be conscious and consistently aware. You intentionally insulate yourself from the possibility of losing belief in what you have and will accomplish.

Next is the Moderate Approach, which simply means you are aware that 'seeking to fail' exists. You decide to stay conscious by accepting the challenge to read, study and apply lessons learned along your way. But you decide not to worry about the people in your life who are negative in their outlook and approach to business, and maybe even life. They still surround you more than anyone else. You believe you owe them, based on your relationships. You feel you'll be alright despite the constant, unsure language that surrounds you.

Finally, there is the Passive Approach, which is not really an approach. You have heard 'seeking to fail' can happen, but you aren't concerned about it ever affecting you. The people and places that surround you are not your concern. The impact of negative relationships in your life is not your concern.

Leaders and trailblazers face this real line in the sand every day. The decisions you make along your journey have an everlasting impact on whether you seek to fail. Focus on preventative measures, which are real solutions for long term success.

Below are three practices that can keep your business ship floating for years to come.

Begin with an activity that complements your mental approach to winning—personal development. If there is any one thing I attribute most of my success to, it is this easy yet underutilized activity. It gave me the push to figure out the how-tos when challenges arose for myself and the people who looked up to me.

Personally developing involves reading books, watching videos, listening to lessons and attending seminars that share success principles. It is personally earned, and you can now apply book knowledge and common sense to arrive at a solution. I am not saying you no longer have to ask a mentor for assistance. As you build, you will continue to seek guidance. However, your need to request assistance will lessen as you begin to find solutions on your own. As a result, the questions you ask are no longer basic level and can be focused on leadership and development.

Next, surround yourself with people who raise you up. I will always remember pouring my heart out at a national event in front of tens of thousands of people. I gave it my all, and I had prepared for this event as if everything depended on it. And coming offstage, I felt great. I heard the applause, the cheering and my name being chanted. In the hallway going back to my seat, I ran into a group of people who stopped me to ask a question about leadership. At first, I thought about how exhausted I was. I started to ask them to email me so I could respond after the session. I really wanted to relax. Then Leadership 101 kicked in, and I thought, "No, answer their question. Responding to their needs is what a leader does."

They asked me what enabled me to know what to do in a tough situation. No one had ever asked me that, but I only had to think for a moment. I told them that one of the key components to my success was surrounding myself with great people. People better than myself. Because of that, my lid was raised, and my success was the sum total of the people I surrounded myself with.

My subconscious knew this, but I had never shared it before. They said they were amazed I would admit that in public—making my point. I told them when you surround yourself with greatness, you have no problem sharing credit and taking responsibility instead of placing blame. In essence, I wasn't admitting anything. I was honoring the impact that great people had on my past, present and future! I was leading by example and assisting in their present and future success!

Rule #20 - Whatever you give away, double will come back.

Have you ever noticed what happens to most people who win the lottery? They go from an average income to millionaires overnight. The people they know, the press, everyone seems to wish they had their winnings. A few years go by, and many are economically right back where they started. Most people say, "How could that happen? It will never happen to me." But this unfortunate situation can happen to anyone. The lottery winner lost it all because they weren't prepared for good fortune when it arrived. They didn't surround themselves with enough positive people to help make them better. As a result, they don't know what to do with the additional income their winnings brought them.

Personal development and surrounding yourself with people who raise your lid will improve your ability to grow your business, while simultaneously insulating you from seeking to fail.

Finally, be willing to stay active. You'll notice I didn't say stay busy. Active and busy are two different things. You can be busy cleaning your office, updating the computer and looking through office files. You are busy, but you may not be actively building your business. Being active is the process of practicing activities that build your business. As a result, all busy work is not active building. Sharing your business with the same people over and over is busy, but it's not active (productive) behavior. You're busy, no doubt about it. But you're not actively building a new stream of productive business.

To be effective at staying active, carve out a segment called 'Production time' in your schedule. Don't go out and attempt to instinctively grow your business. Be in control and know exactly what your daily focus is. Now you're doing what the best leaders do: You're managing time so you can measure production.

Rule #21 - Begin with the end in mind.

As you launch your business, have a sense of what you want to achieve. If you're not sure, focus on the lifestyle you want to live. If you have monetary needs, focus on a benchmark amount of income. Beginning with what you need and want in mind gives you the ability to goal-set early, and early focus is a key ingredient to long-term success. Being successful means many people want what you're working for or what you have. Remember, this applies to people in the industry as well as prospects that join your organization in the future.

There's an old saying, 'The best drivers don't notice the bumps on the road because they are too busy moving forward.' Have you ever driven quickly down a road? It might have bumps and potholes, but you didn't notice how bad the road was because your mental engagement was all about getting to your destination. How can that be? Your intelligence level hasn't changed, and your car hasn't gotten any better. The only difference is your focus is on your mental decision to arrive. This same phenomenon is true in your business. Keep your focus on the destination and the task along the way to arrive at the time you desired.

If you lose focus by watching and comparing yourself to others, you'll slow down. Then, instead of looking at your

'NETWORK' TO W.I.N. (DECIDE NOT TO IMPLODE)

destination, you'll become distracted by the bumps and potholes. I was with a leadership group years ago, and one of the participants said, "If you don't watch what others are doing, you might miss something important." I agreed that you 'may' miss something. Then I asked the group if any of them had ever been on the freeway stuck in bumper-to-bumper traffic. You're stuck and can't move to your exit that's just two short miles ahead. The impact of an accident, broken vehicle or something else impeding a smooth, safe trip has attracted everyone's attention. Their minds are no longer on the destination they were working toward. As a result, the delay has impacted their ability to arrive where they wanted to be at the time they anticipated.

There is no difference in business building. Spend your time watching everyone else, and you can lose sight of where you were striving to go. When you're actively building your business, moving forward on your success road, you should spend more time in production mode and less time being simply busy. The most effective way to accomplish this is to have a plan and work it. Your plan is your schedule, and your schedule is your roadmap.

It is important to stay in active mode, even if you have achieved more than you ever thought possible. Continue doing what you originally did to become successful. The best leaders mentally trick themselves into always believing the next level is the best level. They do this because first, they know they can't afford to feel like they've arrived at a final destination. Thinking this way is counterproductive to ever realizing new goals are out there. Next, the best leaders know the more success they have, the more lives they will impact.

Make personal development, surrounding yourself with positive people who lift your lid, and staying active a part of your everyday routine. Stay positive even when things are not going as planned. Even when it seems like everything is just not working, stay positive with your mindset and activities.

Rule #22 - Bad news is shared with your mentor, sponsor or someone in your organizational structure above you. Good news gets shared with everyone in your organization.

This basic rule can help you avoid carelessness that can implode your business. Keep your organization moving forward, excited, focused and driven. When you begin sharing negative things that may have happened to one or two people, you are no longer motivating your organization's people. As a matter of fact, negative news can have a demotivating impact on them. So, ensure you protect your organization by keeping them motivated to win, not motivated to gossip about everything that doesn't go right. I guarantee there will be a few things that don't go right on your way to creating success. That's a byproduct of building a business. Don't stay worried about them; keep moving forward. In the middle of a storm, claim your victory, even when you can't see it. It takes belief and staying active to create success. You will need both to carry you over the hurdles.

Rule #23 - People fail, systems do not.

Most successful organizations thrive on utilizing a time-tested system. A system is a fundamental way of teaching people how certain behaviors will create a predictable outcome. Think about it: When you arrived at your job, you learned how to complete a task. You were taught the system of how things work. It was based on time-tested behavior outcomes (when you do X, you get Y).

When someone new arrived, what did you share when they asked how to complete a task? Most likely, you shared the same system that was shared with you. You knew from experience the predictable positive outcomes when using this system. You and the people in the organization trust the system and share it for sustained positive performance outcomes. Using this system not only tests it, it also produces the results. Networking works the same way. Leaders lessen the chance of inconsistent outcomes by utilizing proven systems that create successful outcomes.

Remember that success gained can quickly become success lost if you unconsciously seek to fail. As the leader, make sure you share systems that have a high degree of positive results for you and the people who are looking to you for guidance.

> *Recap: What we say often becomes reality. Leaders speak positive expectations because negative language encourages a 'seek to fail' mentality in the leader and others they influence.*
>
> *When you must discuss a setback, share it with your upline support network. The good news can and should be shared with everyone.*
>
> *Anticipate successful endeavors, and don't worry about the speed bumps that appear on everyone's road.*

CHAPTER 7

'Network' Is an Ongoing Process! (Choosing your successors)

Let's discuss the difference between mentorship and successorship. It's been said that you will automatically have successors when you take the time to mentor. Defining successorship as a byproduct of mentorship is possible but not always accurate.

You may mentor one, five or even hundreds of people over the course of your career. How many of these people you share business development time with will you choose to succeed you? Potential successors don't always arrive with an heir apparent name tag. A successor is someone you're not just teaching how to be successful; you're modeling how they can eventually become impactful!

As you begin Networking, you have decided what company you are going to enroll in. You now understand there's a legacy of people who will pour into you. You've built up a level of belief and trust in them, and as a result, they develop a level of trust in you. You know the importance of being diligent, not careless and the impact of not imploding. What's left for you now is implementing a strategy to carry on what has been passed on to you. You accomplish this when you share what you've learned with others. Mentoring others and picking a successor are the keys to achieving this goal.

Mentorship empowers you to make a lasting impact on our industry for years to come. Decades from now, others may still feel your positive impact when all that remains is your legacy. Imagine making an impact so great that your legend lasts longer than your lifespan! Mentorship happens when someone with knowledge of how to achieve a task stays with the people they are training through the learning process up to the mastery level. There's a big difference between teaching and being a mentor. I can get in front of a room and teach how to accomplish a task. When I mentor, however, I teach and share how to successfully accomplish a goal. I'm with you as you implement strategies and eventually master the process. Mentorship is key to long-lasting success in your organizations and our industry.

'NETWORK' IS AN ONGOING PROCESS! (CHOOSING YOUR SUCCESSORS)

So, how do you choose who to mentor? Begin by making a conscious decision to work with the willing. A willing student wants what you have to share. Often you'll see something in them that shows their willingness to expand and then share with others. That's what happened in my career and has been instrumental in my success. My early mentors saw my desire to learn and my willingness to reach back and share information with others. They were correct to share with me because of what they saw in me. As a result, I've been empowered to share information with thousands who are willing and receptive to learning.

When you invest time with the willing, it minimizes wasted time. When you recognize someone with these characteristics, your desire to mentor will arise. It matters not if you work with them personally or spot them in a crowded auditorium.

There are a few traits to look for when choosing who to mentor. One of the most obvious is, they ask questions. They don't sit on their hands, waiting for someone else to ask the question that they really need answered. Next, take notice of the note-takers. They appreciate the information and the time you're spending with them; they don't waste an opportunity to learn. They will often come out and ask you to train or work with them. Some leaders may see this as a burden when someone is not in their direct line of sponsorship. Remember what we said about receiving double after you give, and make decisions to help others based on their willingness to learn and their desire to share with others.

Never forget what we said earlier: A leader is 24/7. You're always on. Like so many other leaders, I've helped people who are not in my line of sponsorship. When people in my organization witnessed this, it had a positive impact on those who were willing to learn. They now understood they, too, should share positive learning with the deserving along the way to their success.

Passing on the torch of understanding is one of the most enjoyable parts of being a successful networker.

When someone wants what you have or wants you to teach them how to be greater than you (surrounding yourself with greatness), this is one of the most rewarding parts of the industry! In our industry, Giving is living!

The combination of others wanting what you have, and your willingness to give, is the key to your legacy living on. The importance of creating your legacy is the reason I left this topic for the final chapter. Legacies in this industry have created dynasties and are a key to industry growth. Knowing others who will be even better than the giants

'NETWORK' IS AN ONGOING PROCESS! (CHOOSING YOUR SUCCESSORS)

that came before you generates smiles, happiness and hope for the future of our industry.

Traditional business breeds secrecy and favors to gain access to needed information to advance. When a leader is hesitant to share, it has a detrimental effect on all. The leader thrives in an environment where they're looking great because others appear ordinary or marginal. In traditional business, I haven't seen the willingness to share success information. What I've seen is a perceived threat that the success of others is going to take what belongs to the leader. As a result, decisions are consistently made not to mentor (this is called a crabs in a barrel mentality). Traditional business leaders often decide not to share success stories, tips, anecdotes and facts. Instead of having a sharing outlook, the corporate environment breeds a mentality of scarcity. In traditional business, this mentality lives at every level of leadership. It's difficult to put a label on this type of thinking, so I will label it 'Non-network' thinking.

Let's talk about successorship. If you were to leave your organization, whether you retired or suddenly left, who would you want to continue effectively leading in your absence? This is what successorship is all about. It simply means you put emphasis and importance on proper preparation. You anticipate the reality of the organization without you being present.

READY, SET, NETWORK

What characteristics do you look for in your successor? Picking your successor is not about someone's traits; it's often about you. Don't worry if you've never built a business before. As you build your success story, you'll learn to follow and trust your instincts. People you meet will remind you of someone who mentored you, someone who left an indelible imprint on your success journey. I want to share an example of someone who thought about the future of his company and the positive impact his preparation had on the company.

In August of 1980, Coca-Cola named Mr. Roberto Goizueta the company's new CEO. Mr. Goizueta is considered one of the most dynamic leaders in the history of Coke. He introduced Diet, Cherry and New Coke. He was also the CEO when Coke made several billion-dollar transactions with other companies, sending the company's bottom line to record highs. He was an incredibly progressive leader, and Coke had unprecedented growth numbers under his leadership.

With all of his accomplishments, he is most known for his attention to preparation. Mr. Goizueta passed away suddenly in 1997 from lung cancer. Mr. Goizueta's greatest contribution was his ability to select, groom and mentor his successor, M. Douglas Ivester. As a result, his proper preparation resulted in continued success. He's an example

'NETWORK' IS AN ONGOING PROCESS! (CHOOSING YOUR SUCCESSORS)

of someone's success and legend outliving them. Because he understood the importance of successorship, Coke continued to grow and flourish, never missing a step.

Mr. Goizueta's story is symbolic of the importance of picking your successor. Decide today that your organization is spearheaded by you, a leader who majors in preparation for the future. Deciding to choose a successor will determine if your organization will have a short history of success or become legendary. It does not matter that you may not run a billion-dollar business like Coca-Cola. Do not think in terms of size or production of the company. Instead, focus on how many lives you and your organization impact now and in the future. Long-term business success changes lives. Successor preparation empowers your organization to have a legendary impact on the lives of many. All this happened because you decided to choose a successor

One more point to remember. Deciding to choose a successor puts you in a category of visionaries. Just remember not to complicate the process. The task of picking your successor requires two things: a willingness to choose and remembering the lessons you absorbed along the way as you grew in the industry. In short, you are looking for people who remind you of your career mentors and you.

Decide today your name, success and legend will live on like Mr. Goizueta. Leave your mark on the distributors and prospects you'll impact over your time in this industry.

> *Recap: Now you're Ready, Set and Networking. Remember to look around with purpose for who has earned your mentorship.*
>
> *Along the way, someone will stand out as the special student of the business who should carry on your legacy of leadership. Choose wisely.*
>
> *Keep the process simple and streamlined. A good feeling about someone is probably an indicator to mentor and possibly choose your successor.*

'NETWORK' IS AN ONGOING PROCESS! (CHOOSING YOUR SUCCESSORS)

Now, go out and build your story that motivates others. Create a story that will inspire a networker to find time and income freedom. Believe in you and the positive impact you'll create, and get it done!

All My Best!

www.ingramcontent.com/pod-product-compliance
Lightning Source LLC
Chambersburg PA
CBHW021130080526
44587CB00012B/1209